A TASTE

A TASTE

POEMS

Morty Schiff

Pleasure Boat Studio: A Literary Press
New York

A Taste © 2013 by Morty Schiff

All rights reserved. This book may not be reproduced, in whole or part, in any form, except by reviewers, without the written permission of the publisher.

ISBN 978-1-929355-91-4
Library of Congress Control Number: 2013900130

Interior design by Susan Ramundo
Cover design by Laura Tolkow, Flushleft
Cover art by Ralph Martel, after Albrecht Dürer, "Four Riders of the Apocalypse"

Pleasure Boat Studio books are available through your local bookstore, or through the following:
SPD (Small Press Distribution)
Partners/West
Baker & Taylor
Ingram
Amazon.com and **bn.com**

and through
PLEASURE BOAT STUDIO: A LITERARY PRESS
www.pleasureboatstudio.com
201 West 89th Street
New York, NY 10024

Contact **Jack Estes**
Fax: 413-677-0085
Email: pleasboat@nyc.rr.com

DEDICATION

for Rebecca, Amalia, Danisa

A crushed sparrow could make your heart jump out of your mouth.
—Yiyun Li

. . . the poems you would
have written had
your life been good.
—W.H. Auden

CONTENTS

I. Allegro ma non troppo
Conversation 1
If It Please, Oblivion (and Other Cartesian Obsessions) 2
Conversation II 3
A Taste 4
Love Song 5
A Jet Plane Crashes into a Secluded Convent 7
time turned 8
Bird Nest with Young 10
Marcel's Author Eschews Praise When It's Deserved,
    Delights in It When Not (in Old Age) 11
Delia's Gone 12
A Crushed Sparrow Could Make Your Heart Jump out of Your Mouth 13
Study in Green, Darkly 14
Tale of Two Muses 15

II. Adagio
Invoking Your Name in Order to Live in Eternity's Sunrise 17
Ant 19
"Poetry Should be at Least as Well Written as Prose" 20
The Boy 21
The Boy II 23
Sweet William 24
Honor Roll in the Hay 25
night verse 26
Green Peppers 27
Michelangelo's "David" 28
a prayer 29
The Infinite Regress of Separate Ways 30
Reason for a Thousand Disputes Ontological, Epistemological,
    and Other 31
Demonstrating the Continuity of Your Existence During
    Periods of Absence 32

Winter in Paris 36
Mosquito 37

III. Scherzo: Presto

Music and Time 39
Sleep and Poetry 40
disjunctive clauses 41
Bagatelle for a May Night 42
Cartesian Taste 43
Ballade 44
Lunar Landing 45
Apparition 47
The Zone 48
The Darwin Suite 49
    I.   Double Helix and High Water
    II.   Ballad of Sorts of the Just So Genitalia
    III. A Comment, upon Visiting an Anatomy Museum, on the Blind Watchmaker's Putative Ability to Produce, Give or Take a Billion Years, a Full Human Being Replete with Central Nervous System, Blood Circulation Network, Body Musculature, Kidneys, Liver, Heart, Etc.
    IV. My End is My Beginning
    V.   Spider
    VI. Nightmare
Columbine 53
Bloom's Brothel Blues 55
glas 56
Dirge 57
Le Poème de Prévert 58
The Prévert Poem 59
jeu d'eaux 60
water play 62
l'esprit de l'escalier 64
Harlequin 65
Homage to Avram Reisin 66
Homage to Avram Reisin II 67
Seven at Seventy 68

    I. Transition
    II. What Did You Make of the Dream
    III. The Bird
    IV. Beckett
    V. The Writer Looks at Himself and Blinks
    VI. From Dylan T. to B. Dylan
    VII. Memory

IV. Trio: Andante Sustenuto

Liebstod	73
Variation on the Liar Paradox Composed on Seeing in the Movies Blood Gush Like a Fountain from the Temple of a Viet Cong Captive Shot Cold Bloodedly at Very Close Range	74
Fugue on an August Evening	75
Song for *The End of the Affair*	76
Watching *Woyzek*	77
Waiting for the Veil to Be Lifted	78
Reflections in a Jaundiced Eye	79
T.S., W.B., and The Beatles Answer Present at the Umpteenth Coming	80
Ars Poetica cum Apologia Pro Vitae Summa	81
The World Is Everything	82
"What Good is 'I Love You' If It's the Answer to a Question?"	83
Lucia	84
The Tongue at the Tower of Babel	85
Thank You, Roger Kimball, Thank You, Martin Filler, Respectively	86
"The Lottery" Revisited	87
Memorabilia	88
Bio	89

V. Allegretto

On Science and Art	91
"The Free Man Thinks of Nothing Less Than of Death"	93
Port-au-Prince, January 2010	94

    I. *Terra Firma*
    II. African Friend

    III. Voltaire
    IV. Buddha Visits Haiti
Crazy Jane, Demotic 97
Mr. Scott of Oakley Street, London 98
The J, K, L Suite 99
The Marvin Story 102
Momento Mori 103
Macbeth Doth Murder 104
Short Story 105
Mother 106
Afterthought 107
The Nature of Things 108
A Back Roads Route to Keats's Grand Concordance 109
Bagatelle in a Minor Key 110
Plainly Said 111

About the Author 113

I. Allegro ma non troppo

Conversation

I caught the perfect bubbles that you blew
Between your words against my staring eyes,
And in the burst of dampness came a clue
To deal with leaden grammars in disguise.

Dazzled, I went on to ask the mist
That thickened as the captive bubbles kissed
And died in a wet, funereal swoon
Whether, in such an age as this, the moon

In all its cool, yellow extravagance
Was also catchable like this, like this
A message past the one of synthesis,
Caged in bubbles bursting all by chance.

If It Please, Oblivion (and Other Cartesian Obsessions)

if it please, oblivion
just what was it I was thinking
thinking no longer
the fright stopping everything
the coffin lid tight
cramped arms
pinned sides
what a death that would be—
and then the stupidity of
losing that $800 check
again a jab in the gut
shame here as painful as existential dread
what was it I thought and
wanted not to think about
not to think about

Conversation II

Stationed at the window seat, arms folded,
you gazed into the dusk. Sunday, five o'clock.
Outside, New York was choked with litter.
I leaned my cheek against my hand,
engaged your gaze across the room,
and surrendered by treasonable degrees
to the determination, now that it was autumn,
to reconvene the seminar of love—
anything to perpetuate, after a fashion,
the summer's tenderness.

—Philosophical regress of a sort
informs the hurdy gurdiest of tunes;
and simple pleas of disengagement,
coolly worded, speckled with references
to the mutual good, arouse. I'm sorry,
what I say now is not meant to arouse.
What I just said was not meant to arouse.
What I had said—Then kindly choose,
you interrupted, your palindromes
with less deliberation . . .

Far better than I you understood
the perils of explication.
You said, Call again when this fever desists.
I wavered. I dangled new conciliatory images
before my inner eye. I would have launched
a gaggle of plumed sounds had you let me.
You favored no such corruption.
You crossed your legs and bit your lip.
I shuddered to think of the crowded intentions
animating the wannest word I lugged
from my lover's arsenal.

A Taste

A friend, poor girl, herself ravaged,
Whom I mentioned the title
Of the book to, said,
Mainliners, the needle in,
Say when the smack's good
You can almost taste it . . .
While I had in mind only that
It's the same word
The same idea in every semantic,
Goût, Geschmack, Gusto,
Standing for, what else,
taste
In food, clothes, music, pictures, poems,
You like it, swallow!
You don't, spit it out!
Rhetorically speaking
Where would taste be without
The autonomic reflex of the tongue,
The tongue having spoken?

Love Song

You are joy, first,
        to hold, stare at, be with,
then a memory of pain,
shades of an earlier history
        imperfectly interred.
I pay for ecstasy with anxiety
as gunshy I lightly tread
        in your presence,
avoiding the gestures
it would be doom to repeat.

You are, to look into your eyes,
        a mystery
        deeper than the night.
I want to solve you
and lay the parts of you out
        on each side
        of a balanced equation,
I consult my answer book
        but you're not in it.

You've invaded my mind
        like an army bent on conquest,
driving out the clutter of trivia
        that squatted there.
I fix on you
        as the center of consciousness
the hub all spokes lead to,
the first thought in anything.

Yet all that's nothing compared
        to your occupation
        of my senses.
the heart does not take orders
but sometimes it obeys:

I smell one smell,
I taste one taste,
      et cetera,
I hear one sound—
      your silence
determining the rhythm of my being.

A Jet Plane Crashes into a Secluded Convent

"My Lord did the miracle of the loaves,"
A nun whispers, and rubs the heavy beads,
Her heaven's jewelry. Beside, the blue green leaves
Flutter on the convent walls, her faith's defense
Against the age's thrust, while miracle wine
Spills crimson on her nun's black, and feeds
The ardor of her artless virgin sense.

She hadn't reckoned heaven a source of fright—
A shooting bird whose parabolic line
Transfigures the air and in a blind of fire
Dashes the home of simple nuns, and signs
Ten charred holy corpses to the first light.
No nun had reckoned miracles require
Measureless grief, a morbid morning rite.

time turned
—thoughts on the film *2001, a Space Odyssey*

liken comprehensible history
to a spot light
trilling the time line
shining more forward than back

the point is
we lose a thing or two as we
move forward
as only a finite span stays lit
the dimness
never far behind

so science fiction's constructs
those freewheeling future fabulations
seem paradoxically more familiar
in the lovely sense of that word
i.e., I *know* you
than
let us say

a Louis XVI chair
its strange design
truly unknowable now
in either intent or execution

and in some twist
of effect and cause
with time itself undone
the object's found
the how and why forgotten

so the pyramids
darkly recede
while time to come is embraced
and lived as though
as the French say
already seen

Bird Nest with Young

Perhaps it is that all-thinking man too
Is sorry, sorry as the bird whose
Nest an angry summer rain attacks, and builds his
Stony mansion quite by native accident
Where silver waters wash the river bottom

This warm bird's talent, unnumbered though
Symmetrical, shapes from homeless twine and
Ancient yellow grasas a circle of ardent life
Where oval eggs are blue andblood is coloured fire,
Where summer flirts with time awhile before
The blood of this sad bird washes rthe dusky sk.

Perhaps the truth to man is here, among
The sorry mouths of birds so young,
So unaware, they live by appetitie alone
And sing for food although they cannot fly;
But bird blood courses like desire, and
Feathers will swarm their sik skin wings
Before this tree with green will slough its mobile fruit.

Perhaps man's life is just this summer rhythm,
Bird life and bird death, big-mouthed
Bird hunger of the young, nothing more;
Man nust be gladder living bird time—
Time of fire, no subtle ash of memory:
Or has man thought of this before,
Before the drumof this man's song,
Considered it before he denied the bird
To strive for something to outdistance happy sorrow?

Marcel's Author Eschews Praise When It's Deserved, Delights in It When Not (in Old Age)

Ruminations courtesy of Marcel Proust
about how hoary Bergotte came to roost
he who (a vivid tableau tumbles down the years)
for years and years and laborious days
pooh poohed the praise
from hangers on
his early writings won.
Is there such a thing as genuine humility?
Yes, Bergotte's . . .
It kept him free.
Much later with invention failing
and onset aging fears
still punching out novels, flailing
hoary Bergotte sops up lots
of accolades
showered on him by sycophants
and stylish maids
in a courtly dance
or country reel
for work unworthy of them—
all told, a convoluted theme
worthy of Proust, Marcel
a story I feel
compelled to tell
and retell.

Delia's Gone

Frail Delia whirled in modern dance, and led you
To expect the grace of her limbs to entertain
All portions of her rhythmic body; or she might
Have you, so observing, test the supple muscle
Beneath her skin—though my hand's music chided,
This was the belly Carl touched for love
And I for humor.

The gestures of her lover betrayed a happy guy
Who often grinned indifferently: for her part Delia
Found no delight except perhaps in pain and telling
How he almost knowingly used her to a sad purpose:
Consoling her I used to take her hand, remembering
These were the fingers Carl touched for love
And I for humor.

Now when she died no sky was sympathetic, no scattered
Leaves went brown: a mere disease attacked her, happened
To have won. Mourning her was painful and the steady
Occupation of those she'd known, while Carl, too,
Stayed glum. With a knowing smile I settled that
There died a heart Carl touched for love
And I for humor.

Ultimately, though, he broke down and dropped
The proper tears. He stared and gripped his head
In an endless muttering of her name, so
Miserable in the loss, so empty less his Delia.
I was a spectator to the event, recalling
The slender billfold Carl touched for love
And I for humor.

"A Crushed Sparrow Could Make Your Heart Jump out of Your Mouth"
—Yiyun Li

A crushed sparrow could make
Your heart jump out of your mouth.
Ditto, for goodness sake
(I am, therefore I think),
The hairy crawler of myth
Quashed in the kitchen sink.

Study in Green, Darkly

I somehow guessed that alleys were
Behind the green roads lined with fir
And carried down their alley ways
The awkward longing that dismays.

I have a forest of a brain,
Envy leaps green down every lane
And chokes the passage of simple truth,
Detritus of a misspent youth.

The traveler grown cannot break free,
Green bends his neck precariously,
Never can he set apart
The restless taunting of his heart.

Tale of Two Muses
—for Louis Phillips

Ed's muse
Waylaid him early on
In teenage party passageways
Waking lovelorn
The broken pieces of his heart
Strewn underfoot on the naked floor.
She sang poignantly as to make a listener weep
And when with time the shattered pieces mended
As suddenly as she began
As soon stopped singing.

Ned's muse
Stirred as she was
By human suffering *tout court**
Thrummed an inexhaustible melody
Of pain, mastectomy, and loss.
Time unfolding furnished her
Examples of essential misfortune of every kind
And, catastrophe her trope,
She plaintively plainspokenly
Sang on.

*French: that and that alone.

II. Adagio

Invoking Your Name in Order to Live in Eternity's Sunrise
"He who kisses the joy as it flies / Lives in . . ."
—Blake

So might a module—heart or spaceship—
If flighted right, course an astral trajectory
that leaves behind the diurnal rhythms

to enter a realm of ever sunrise,
achieving not stasis but a wild careening,
a furious hanging on despite the galactic wind,

like riding a comet whipping around a star,
to the accompaniment of clanging music and
infrared pyrotechnics played on the fullness of space.

Below we ride broncos and hang on for dear life.
Yet earthly meetings can wreak havoc to the sky,
to time, and to all the other fixtures of the cosmos,

make the obscured red sunball climax rhythmically
as it moves like a swollen boil on the planet's rim,
while tongues of solar fire, perfectly suited

to our terrestrial doings, lick at the corona.
Below our mingled limbs claw to find a fit,
a celestial motion regulated to catch

the sun spilling on the threshold of becoming,
igniting the globe degree by longitudinal degree,
ball on ball, Bevs of energy sparking off our flanks. . . .

And all because you timed your kisses just right.
The warp of eternity couches in our exploding loins,
for if you soared on the edge of that explosion,

moving like smithereens at the shock wave's front,
time would be suspended as you soared
and our mad embrace matched in the starry chaos.

Ant

The Anthropomorphic
Principle aside
or maybe stage center
what is it producing
a pang as I pursue
the scuttling ant
speeding up
turning this way that way
in a bid to outrace me
despite the guaranteed outcome
nonetheless of
its being obliterated
it being no match for
my Brobdingnagian thumb?

"Poetry Should be at Least as Well Written as Prose"
—Ezra Pound

I tried, Ezra, I really did, and then again, the whispery feeling it's all summed up in, in the instantaneously transitional time of the moment, this second, the dish crashing to the tiled floor, the pain in the gut for no reason other than the butter stain on the trousers, the elation of finding at long last (a half hour later) the lost letter exactly placed where last left a long half hour ago . . . yes, and oh the overwhelming spontaneous screaming loud on learning that, I hesitate to tell you, Lorraine died the other day, I saw the obit in *The Times* . . .

The Boy

The boy was *serious*, no shit. Maybe
He didn't actually see a wolf
Crouching in the bushes a hundred feet away
But it sure seemed like it
And he in charge of a dozen sheep
Each one precious, animate, lovable
And so he did what you or I would do
Cried as loud as he could—Wolf!

Came running a dozen shtarkers with shotguns
Looked around, decent guys, really
Thorough as firemen, who finally said
You're mistaken, kid, no wolf here
Make sure next time before you panic

The boy felt chastised, swore
He'd never do such an embarrassing thing again
No prankster he, just stressfully
Living with a sense of doom impending
The catastrophe, the certain catastrophe
Coming when least expected—but when?

And when as soon as the following night
He was sure he saw a wolf where he only thought
There was one the day before, what could he do but
Scream loudly into the darkened sky—Wolf!

They came even faster this time, the men
Guns at the re, looked everywhere
Tore the protective bushes down, found nothing
Left even faster, everything faster, pretty disgusted
With nothing but a quick backward glance
More devastating than reproachful words
The boy who'd duped them twice

The third night the wolf strolled into the yard
Did he come from behind the bush? Hard to tell. . . .
Whatever, he calmly walked among the sheep
The sheep ignored him for the time being
You know, kept on grazing, the way sheep are
The way sheep do even with the slaughterer at hand
The boy though freaked out
He screamed a couple of times, each time a little louder
He hurt his throat, his voice gave out
No one came
You desperately wish it weren't so
The ending is the familiar one you know.

The Boy: A Sonnet

The boy was *serious*, no shit. Maybe
He didn't actually see a wolf. He *thought*
He did. He did what anyone would quickly
Do. He cried Wolf. And lo, he promptly got

A response. They came, the men, in swarms.
They searched everywhere, thorough as firemen,
But no wolf. Evidently a false alarm.
Kid, make sure you see before you scream again!

Ashamed but sure day two 'twas a wolf he saw
He screamed. Men came, looked, left, sensing betrayal.
Next day the wolf . . . came, strolled with gaping jaw.
Again the boy cried Wolf!—to no avail.

You desperately wish it weren't so,
The ending is the familiar one you know.

Sweet William

Puzzled Will found his will puzzled
When he saw no traveler returned . . .

Life wasn't what he'd thought.
Unduly spurned
He posed the question iambically
Whether to be
Or not.

Honor Roll in the Hay

You thrilled me listing the women I've kissed,
    If that was your intention,
I thrilled concocting the longer list
    Of names you did not mention.

Names tripping on the tip of my tongue
    Ladies I knew well,
I'd gladly recall them in rhyme and song
    But I practice kiss, don't tell—

Don't tell, unless the deft reply
    Skirts what it abjures,
Both gives and hides the name on the sly
    By listing it as "Yours."

night verse

love, we weave out of the moods of the night
such kinds of blankets, lace, and shawls
transparent as our nakedness, smooth as the lips
we join and unjoin within these four walls

the kiss we share has the name of kiss
the taste of languor; and smells intrude
to stop the brains that measure in their cells
like time calipers the span of this attitude

the lamp your skin glows by doesn't alter
the pleasurepain contact in the night's middle
lets fuse these bodies confused with penetration
though tongues and eyes contribute to a riddle

real and dream mix in our limbs of tangle
instruments of love abstract as love's liver
but what in the embrace leads to exhaustion—
what is the relation to receiver of giver?

to griever of lover? to desire of death?
hearts pounding madly in the night's cover
we spangle the darkness with our crooked caress
honor giver as donor though receiver is lover

Green Peppers

Green peppers purge the mouth
a poet might declare
encapsulate a truth
in the apt metaphor

differing from the man
of science in just this
who will request a chem-
ical analysis

Michelangelo's "David"

put away for a moment the magnificent
couched tension
in the limbs
The muscles starting in the buttocks
and rippling down the legs
the parts and postures of young manhood
caught and held in stone timeless
as the stars
put away those secrets stone carvers
knew from early on that Michelangelo uses also
and fix on David's eyes
blazing away with such fierce intensity
they live
there's an audacity in modeling eyes
that most liquid piece of body work
to try to seize in the coldest of materials
all the mystery that eyes divulge of humans
their thoughts their motives their crazy passions
all the puzzling beauty of their souls
I know this boy
the sculptor seems to say
and yet I do not know him
for every work's a celebration in a way
of what we do not know
of what we feel because we do not know

a prayer
      —for Nance Sommerschild)

I do not know
whether febrile faith
is not foremost
cerebration
with untold awe
of the world
of the word

I do not know
whether febrile words
are not in fact
in their moral might
the whip of conscience
the time wrought stayer
of the hand

but I know no
lustered thought ever
left the teeming mind
not enfolded
in a fleeting sound
plucked from a
heavenly lyre

The Infinite Regress of Separate Ways

I no longer find it necessary
to tell you that

I no longer find it necessary
to tell you that

I

Reason for a Thousand Disputes Ontological, Epistemological, and Other
—for Michel Pical

Belief lies in the tissue,
Not the issue.

Demonstrating the Continuity of Your Existence During Periods of Absence

one twentieth of a second
catching 24 movie screen images per second
the liar brain prepares a continuum
though ultimately movement and time
like energy may be discrete
stepped in truth ;like a jerking second hand
yetr the residual visual preserves like an ember
the irregular light on the brain's cellular screen
now reality lies somewhere in between
the cellular screen and the movie screen
and I'm faithlessly made aware
of the epistemological consequences of an eyeblink
your frightening disappearance as my eyelid
drops and lifts in a twentieth of a second
for the eye's relief not mine
looking at something less precious
the eye is quicker than the mind
but you so suffuse my thinking that with you
the brain works faster than the eye can blink
and you disappear regularly
your reappearance before my uncurtaining eye
not quite sufficient to prevent
a heart pang as you for an instant vanish

one second
the primacy of sight requires you always there
disappearing behind the sweater you're putting on
your head leaves leaving the rest of your body an
imperfect testimony to your continued presence
a second of time is sufficient for disaster
but your hands adroitly pull you through
and I wise like Zeno follow your heads trajectory

and conclude upon your safe return
taking into account all movements
and all absences that
seeing you at A at time B and at C at time D
you were at all times somewhere in between
against my darker fears
restored to tranquility my mind in a finite time
fuses a memory molecule to memorialize
your annihilation and re-creation in my sight

five hours
is every hour just the seconds in it
does not a principle of emergence beyond counting
prevail in this appalling separation
you spin out of orbit out of sight
you return independent
recognized by a despairing mind
I wonder are you the same when you return
have you not floated through unusual spaces
undergone molecular change
isn't the world created anew each instant
and what of the parts that have lost sight of each other
for five (5) hours (hrs.)
and do you as we reenter each other's sphere
find it at all necessary
after your autonomic locomotions in my absence
to reaffirm my existence reaffirming yours

overnight
waking to wonder who I am
checking walls bed bed partner name
looking with reassurance at you
my memory of you no less a clue than mine of me
I hold you close and close my eyes

we total and mirror the things around us
we count on the memory of objects ion the roomscape
to redefine ourselves in time and space
meantime you've wandered in Lethean realms
dreaming wildly with or without me
traveled beyond behind your lidded eyes
intoxicated by sleep warmth I observe
this is the bed of morning
and if you are new so am I

three days
time enough for another lover
to have bitten your neck
inhaled exhaled your breath
shaped your orifices to his probes
three days is a time of terror
and I watch on you return
in the glass of your eye
the imprint of swoons and looks directed
at the other the other lover
then you continue to exist
as a wound in the groin
a spike in the heart
someone else has occupied
your box of sympathies
and scoured my traces out

one month
Descartes preserve us
what are the assurances now of existence
in intermediate history
the creature reappearing
is proof neither of continuity
nor of reincarnation
I have disappeared too

credulity is strained
friends have died
the moon has gone about the earth
where are you and by what (test)
will I know you when you return
eye nose tongue ear finger
you are lodged in a synapse of my brain
but real and dream are not the same

indefinitely
between nothing and grief I will take
trying to make sense of all of this
I'm unable to function cried the patient
you are gone gone
taking half my head with you
reason gone to seed
as I continue to smell you with my mind's eye

Winter in Paris

Dear friend, a better time will visit you
Than these cruel moments you now put up with.
The ghostly rain will dry, the sombre air
Will begin to smell differently, and the strictures

On your heart will ease. I know
The darkness of the city and the smoke
From sidewalk gratings do your melancholy
No good; and it would be insensitive

Not to see they're mood elements
Contributing to the total sadness.
But their gloom is no more reasoned than your
Inner one, or mine. Our despondent equations

Do not vary with the way of the world, or the void
Consequent on the decline of faith; and I see
Nothing looking like a personal defeat
Signing the creases on your brow.

The times are troubled, though, it's true,
And it's a fool who doesn't take seriously
The splayed hares hanging in the butcher shops,
The bloodied rabbits' feet strewn on their floors,

The worried looks one sees in the Luxembourg.
But, dear friend, recall how the senses betray the mind:
You intimidate the angels only when you feel
Logic is the better part of your sorrow.

Mosquito

Puzzled, I suppose. as deeply as I am
by existence, an anxious mosquito keeps
buzzing at my ears, the mood and time
of his busy music largely wrought by leaps
of mind into my blood:
                              but this fellow
shall not drink from me, I declare,
and as he whirs about my head, I follow
with a fatal will the flight he chooses;
the curious strains of his little vampire call
reach out as I slap him in the air
though no real final cadence closes
as he expires between palm and wall.

III. Scherzo: Presto

Music and Time

"Music," he wrote, "is the sole domain
in which man realizes the present."
I never thought Stravinsky would limn
the words for why I always considered
music the longed-for art.
I was thinking of musicians
for whom, as they play,
brain and heart and hands
coordinated in conspiracies of sound,
time becomes the endless moment,
obliterating the traces of past and future.
(O, the sheer physicality of it—
I've seen a string quartet
collectively do a St. Vitus dance
straining for the notes they sought.)
There's a contagious oblivion
to playing in the present,
where memory need only be long enough
to fix the tune
and what vestige exists of time to be
unfolds melodically from the song.
Making and playing are the same
and the music takes its own (sweet) time.

Thus music defines time—
which, it seems, he also said,
though he was thinking no doubt
not of the instrumentalist
but of the composer—the maker that he was,
trying to frame time in a quaverous net.
What then, one may ask,
is the distance between maker and player,
and, can time measure that distance?

Sleep and Poetry

drunk with sleep I dreamt last night
I'd written a poem about Sarah and Julia
that uncannily captured
their languid ways
and their teasing good looks
three stanzas fixed forever
flawlessly typed on a white sheet
read aloud by an aching friend
who glowed as he read each line
because the lines improved with each line
to the very end

in the stern morning
brittle with waking
I had nothing to show
in my overreaching
to indicate that phantom state of grace
except some pedestrian lines
about a dream poem
perfect in another time and space

disjunctive clauses

no grammarian
ever was
or will be
a guru

the linguist's logic
bares
the sentence bones

the prophet's words
percolate
with unparsed promise

Bagatelle for a May Night
—homage to Wallace Stevens

lady loads of belong and bags of own
will not save the free man in his is
a classical look at his burnished I
shows sad as long as have is his

in the day of night in the eye of could
Desire breathes must in the fears of be
may monthly perceives the will of will
in the sad submit of curiosity

O let a generous heart erase the calamity
of indifferent coy and bland appear
love weathers hours in the wallow of won't
and ignores the ever and never that were

and if ear collects but the music in tears
which goldenly answer in space of time
then verses pursue perverse ruses in word
in tracts of abstract in sobs of come

flowers spend as long in the smell of name
as a when's resolve or a mountain rill
as the who of death and the next of expire
the unreal of somewhere and the shadow of real

soar aspires though color weeps tombs
sombre spills decades each right asking when
kiss maintains now though the darkness assumes
and the night whispers why in the teeth of again

lady bellyful of shall in yur moonlong dress
burn truths of incense cluttered with yes
let to feel love and to love decree
and comedian be or be the letter C

Cartesian Taste

I am is my mouth
I am   my mouth
I is   my mouth

Tongue swimming
Cleaving contemplatively
To palate

Ballade

our times together
are gone now
we don't even bother
to ask how

love is a gift
that makes it all possible
art and life
are less able

to sidestep pride
love is a dance
love stands outside
intelligence

and love's mind's more
after all
than bed or dollar
or anything material

love has laws
didn't Alice say that
answer why with why not
and not with because

Lunar Landing

why the cut
of moon
entablatured
over Prince St.(though the building
halving
now quartering it
is surely on
Sullivan)
should divert me now
is partial mystery
partial bore
it's a brisk
November
evening
6:30 pm
and moons over cities
are not supposed
to be top 40 stuff
any longer
but how dismiss
the way that sliver
jerked my blood a little
before I thought of
the risky cultural context
I'm reminded of
how lapsed Catholic Marxist
acolyte Thea
thrilled at learning that
every thought every
feeling came down to a blip
in the
electromagnetic circuitry of the brain
and I
a materialist before I could fuck
have come to gasp

at the mystery of how
just her name whispered in my ear
or even that piece of moon
can so set
the matter of my mind going

Apparition

kissing your face
after what seems like years
I'm a prospector in the field
undaunted by the fool's gold
in your folds of flesh

sniffing
I'm rather a hog hot after
the hidden truffles
(your breath gives them away)
of your being

nothing about your body
distastes
I eat the thoughts
implicit in your peerless eyes
I munch on the mood
configured in a curve of thigh

though skin
is the hardest substance to pierce
skin diver I
move toward the mind
that dwells somewhere
in your body's vicinity

Zone

Like that *New Yorker* cartoon
a man reads the paper's obit page
you're looking over his shoulder
and every obit has a headline
your age
two years older
three year younger
it's theater for the reader
the cartoon reader
I look at the man's back and
with no one to look at me I look at myself
this is absurd theater

and yet Will's lines apply
the world's a stage, each must play
though alas the silent actors
whose names are blurred
by the two years older
three years younger headlines
are *not* available for a bow

The Darwin Suite

I. Double Helix and High Water

Francis C. Crick recognized clearly
Even with benign change happening yearly,
Between the cooling of Earth and those telltale fossils
No matter how many times the primordial soup jostles
(This came to him while downing a highball)
There just wasn't time to form a perfectly formed eyeball
In despair he cried out, "Alas and alack!
What else could have kept evolution on track?
I'm loath to give up, I think I'll disinter me a
Theory, though farfetched, called 'Directed Panspermia.'"

II. Ballad of Sorts of the Just So Genitalia:
Kipling, Jaye Gould, and the Leopard's Spots
—for Lynne Belaief

He looked upon her
And found her fair
Never guessing nature
Had fashioned just so genitalia
To accommodate them there.

Beauty in the eye of the beholder
Is a fearful thing to bear
Never guessing nature
Had fashioned just so genitalia
To accommodate them there.

Of the leopard's spots beware
The beast's too swift to care
Or even guess nature
Had fashioned just so genitalia
To accommodate them there.

Selected beyond compare
Such are the private parts we bare
Never outguess nature
That fashioned just so genitalia
To accommodate them there.

Prince, do not despair
The image in the mirror
Never guessed nature
Had fashioned just so genitalia
To accommodate them there.

III. A Comment, upon Visiting an Anatomy Museum, on the Blind
    Watchmaker's Putative Ability to Produce, Give or Take a Billion
    Years, a Full Human Being Replete with Central Nervous System, Blood
    Circulation Network, Body Musculature, Kidneys, Liver, Heart, Etc.

Maybe . . . a Bulova.

IV. My End is My Beginning
            —for David Berlinsky

forget the eyeball
evolution's astonishing
masterpiece that's
now soberly seen as
the neat consequence
of chance and necessity
and contemplate perchance
that other body iris
the lowly low as you can get
anal sphincter

even as you imagine that after
a million years of drizzling shit
into an indifferent universe
mammals acquired
by random mutation and
the sheerest damnable luck
a coiled puckered muscular end
that apparently has endured
in all likelihood because
of its rare adaptational advantage

V. Spider

Spider, arachnid, caught in Darwin's web
An early version of which
wove a web of silk
lookin' mighty purdy
but the flies and wasps and butterflies flew through
even as the web collapsed
and the poor spider died
on the junkheap of species history
at the same time that its wealthy cousin
with parental funds to pay for MIT
graduated and
engineering wise
built a web with struts
flying buttresses more or less
that easily trapped and killed the errant fliers
having the temerity to fly that way
and stuffed on more food it could possibly eat
the fat cat spider reproduced accordingly

VI. Nightmare

Have they grabbed hold
Of nightmares yet? If the tale were told
Survival would be predicated by rights
On post coitally sleeping beside your wife
And having the fright of your life
Rousing you before a bed bug bites

Columbine
        —homage to Paul Verlaine

Leander the lush
Pierrot vaulting a bush
    In a thumb flick
Cassander, old wood
Beneath his monk's hood
    And tunic:

Here's Harlequin, too,
Dandy sharper who,
    His unreal
Dark eyes burning bright,
No mad mask or night
    Can conceal—

Do, mi, sol, mi, re,
What a strange display!
    They laugh, whirl,
They sing, dance, and fall
Led on by a beautiful
    Wicked girl

Whose deceiving eyes
Are green, and catwise
    Shows her charms,
But as soon cries out,
"Away! I'll do without
    Your raised arms!"

Yet they play her sport;
The starry, fated court
    Moves faster—
Oh, toward what, tell,
Melancholy and cruel
    Disaster.

The bad child, all speed,
Will implacably lead
      As she scoops
A rose for her hair,
Her thighs showing bare,
          Her flock of dupes!

Bloom's Brothel Blues

Sing a song of worry
(scrotum full of sperm)
I got myself a honey
soft and fat and warm
with her belly naked
oh I began to sweat
wasn't I forsaken
whose act was incomplete?

glas
—homage to Stevie Smith

(*Leaving at least with one reader the distinct impression of having first been written by the poet in French, Stevie Smith's poem "Dirge" is here retrieved, as it were, in a so-called un- or de-translation.*)

de l'ami d'un ami je goûte l'amitié
de l'ami d'un ami l'amour
mon esprit ahuri
de longues années j'ai lutté
et sais maintenant que jamais
je n'approcherai plus près
que l'ami d'un ami de l'amitié
de l'amour que l'amour d'un ami

vers la nuit sombre
je m'en vais résignée
je n'ai pas si peur de la nuit sombre
que des amis que je ne connais pas
je ne crains pas autant la nuit en haut
que je ne crains les amis en bas

Dirge*
—by Stevie Smith

From a friend's friend I taste friendship,
From a friend's friend love,
My spirit in confusion,
Long years I strove,
But now I know that never
Nearer I shall move,
Than a friend's friend to friendship,
To love than a friend's love.

Into the dark night
Resignedly I go,
I am not so afraid of the dark night
As the friends I do not know,
I do not fear the night above,
As I fear the friends below.

---

*From *Collected Poems of Stevie Smith*, copyright ©1972 by Stevie Smith. Reprinted by permission—along with permission to translate—of New Directions Publishing Corp.

*Le Poème de Prévert**

te souviens-tu amie qui oublie
de m'avoir écrit une carte postale
à l'endroit où il devait se trouver
une laide photo aux couleurs banales
il s'y trouvait profond et clair
un petit poème extrait de Prévert
Grand Bal de Printemps
et maintenant
comme c'est l'hiver
et comme sont rares les vrais amis
je lis et relis
cette carte précaire
mille fois mille fois
pourquoi faire
je ne sais si je n'ai lu plus souvent
les douces paroles écrites par toi
ou le triste poème à l'envers

*In French, translation follows.

The Prévert Poem
—A translation of "*Le Poème de Prévert*"

forgetful friend, do you recall
a touching postcard addressed to me?
There where you'd expect to see
a photograph in dullish hues
you found instead, sure to amuse,
a lovely poem by Jacques Prévert
"Grand Ball for Spring."
Now that winter's here
true friends being rare
I read and reread
your offering
the fragile card
a thousand times
a thousand times
to what end?
not knowing whether
through tears I cried
I oftener read
the words you penned
or the melancholy poem
on the other side

jeu d'eaux*
    —hommage à St.-John Perse (Alexis Léger), Charles Trenet, etc.

l'amère mer mère
mariée aux marées

la mer
femme
en son âme
en sa chair

la mer sévère
adoucie
par les chants
de Perse
St.-John

berce
aussi le coeur
de Charles Trenet
poète de valeur
poète de doux vers
et chansons aimées
moins profonds
que la mer

or la mer
est elle-même
à l'endroit à l'envers
plus superficielle
qu'est dans *Amers*

en strophes allongées
le poète les eaux
Alexis Léger

dont les rythmes s'étendent
comme des vagues propageantes
les vagues les entendent
et l'amère mer chante

*In French, translation follows.

water play
> —homage to St. John Perse (Alexis Leger), Charles Trenet, etc.
> —translation of "*jeux d'eaux*"

the dark mother sea
wedded to the tides

the sea
woman
in body
in soul

the unyielding sea
calmed
by the songs
of Perse
St-John

cradles also the heart
of Charles Trenet
worthy poet
of dulcet verses
and beloved songs
not near deep
as the sea

though the sea itself
churning this way and that
is shallower
far and away
than is, in Amers
in its long verse lines
the poet of the sea
Alexis Leger

whose rhythms expand
like propagating waves
the sea waves listen
and the dark sea sings

l'esprit de l'escalier
—for Bart Midwood

asked at the party
what the name was
of a
clever riposte
suddenly thought of
only afterwards
the party done
and therefore too late
for momentary glory—
he blanked

the witty phrase though
came to him in a flash
as
leaving the party
he like Duchamp's nude
stroboscopically
descended
the staircase

Harlequin

harlequin give your wild deep eyes
deliver your bitten bleeding lips
humble the muscle in your thighs
the hardness in your boned hops

my room tonight say you consent
to ecstasy in the night's cover
these were the words cassander sent
his homosexual lover

the night was black the lamp glowed pale
and shadows moved along the wall
incense smelling and the soft wail
of breathing sounded in the hall

and as they clasped it looked like strife
spilling love along the join
cassander took a glinting knife
and stabbed his lover in the groin

the wound lit up bright as the lamp
harlequin died in slow despair
body limp eyes staring and damp
blood clotting his pubic hair

hand on blade cassander tried
he wrung his hands he mourned his fate
to assuage by suicide
the hate in love the love in hate

Homage to Avram Reisin

A family of eight
Beds only two
When night comes
What do they do

Three sleep with Father
Three sleep with Mother
Hands and feet
Braided together

When night comes
And it's time for bed
Mother begins
To wish she were dead

She means it truly
And no wonder shown
The grave is also narrow
Yet each person lies alone

Homage to Avram Reisin II

when life turns bitter
and your heart writhes in pain
your sad eyes water
to whom do you complain

no matter where or when
everyone has it as bad
I find then solace in my pen
patience in my writing pad

Seven at Seventy

I. Transition

Leaving *à contre coeur**
the Gainsbourg erotic year
for unchartered
septuagenarian terrain
I'm gulpingly made aware
of a pounding refrain
(as I push forward
as though beckoned
by fourscore
into that good night)
that it's already Act the Second
and they don't write
five act plays anymore.

*French, reluctantly

II. What Did You Make of the Dream

What do you make of the dream
First dreamer
Waking in the Ethiopian rift
Four million years ago
Without a theory of dreams
Homo ardipithecus
Without a language
Dreaming in black and white
Waking in a green meadow
Among trees content with no name
Tumbling leafy branches over you
While you dream of your father
Nameless, younger, stronger
Than when you motionless
Put him in a pit

Sand in his gaping mouth
You want to visit the dream again
Say, what did you make of the dream
Dreamed four million years ago
Without a theory of dreams
Without a theory or word for it

Or waking in a room in Bulgaria
A single light bulb suspended
From a high ceiling
Or is it the dream still

What would you make of the dream
Without a theory of dreams

With nothing said about Time
Nameless except the vague notion
A moment had just passed
Where did the moment go

Did the quest for understanding
Begin in the dream
Or in the blinking stars
That when you followed them
Following each other
Regularly . . .

Things change and stay the same
All in the expanse of Time

Brought on as much
By a single light bulb
Suspended from a high ceiling
In a dim lit room in Prague
(or was it Sofia, Bulgaria?)

III. The Bird

Spotted from Goat Island flying by the bay
A grey gull hesitates in flight, alights in the water as though
Cleared by air traffic control—
A bit tired? hungry?—none of these, it's just that
The water looks fine, this patch at least . . .

Two mental states beg. Get me a brain to get me out of here.
Two, give me a bird's brain to know
Deep in my soul
Down to the tips of my delicate webbed feet
Where to land
On water or sand.

IV. Beckett

I ingather the wisdom proffered me
Beckett's I can't go on, I can't go on, I'll go on . . .
Frost's I know only this about life—it goes on!
Stein's deathbed What's the answer / What's the question
And Wittgenstein's Whereof one cannot speak,
One must remain silent.

But still imagining an answer
Offered in a serious talk
Broadcast on the radio
On the news at six o'clock

And early on and never gone
It fatally occurred to me
Most people disdain mystery
And wouldn't turn the radio on

V. The Writer Looks at Himself and Blinks

Showing ignorance
I slip my tongue
In a trance
Left along
Upper lip
To where
Short trip
As though by fate
Upper meets lower
And I slobberingly
Contemplate
The flawless join

And how it might
Have come about
Or otherwise have been
—Allowing me
To humbly speak truth
Shamelessly out
Of the corner
Of my mouth.

VI. From Dylan T. to B. Dylan

These lines I read with a voice
Twice as old as the hand that wrote
I've no intention to revise
And if for me they're bliss to quote
I also note
Again and again
As how
I was bolder then
I'm humbler than that now.

VII. Memory

Memory is like
A Buddha arrow
Bullseyeing when least aimed
Aided maybe by a madeleine
Putting in a wordless word

All, all occurring in
The gelatinous rotunda of the brain
In the swish, swish echo churning
Vociferous chambers of the heart

IV. Trio: Andante Sustenuto

Liebstod

You color my world with what my world lacked—
a center, a purpose death to forestall:
you're my death wish, my death-defying act.

That the things of the world repel and attract
wasn't enough to keep me from a fall
(you color my world with what my world lacked)—

I courted the devil, and made a pact
to clutch the moon though first I had to crawl;
you're my death wish wish, my death-defying act.

For love and death are closely linked, in fact;
I was dying of boredom before your call.
You color my world with what my world lacked,

and I don't expect to quit the world intact:
life's dancers should bear scars after the ball:
you're my death wish, my death-defying act.

I'm dying means, with all my senses wracked,
I'm living the wisest passion of them all,
you color my world with what my world lacked,
you're my death wish, my death-defying act.

Variation on the Liar Paradox Composed on Seeing in the Movies Blood Gush Like a Fountain from the Temple of a Viet Cong Captive Shot Cold Bloodedly at Very Close Range

I will not write this poem

I Will Not Write This Poem

Variation on the Liar Paradox composed on seeing in the
movies blood gush like a fountain from the temple of
a Viet Cong captive shot cold bloodedly at very close
range

Fugue on an August Evening

I saw a dark lady in a dark automobile
Drive aimlessly by the accident,
Car on car, an utter collision.
I walked by in the other direction.

The evening was lit for a neon comedy,
The car on car and the dark lady,
A pizzeria emptied nearby,
A celebration of witness and ceremony.

Hands in pockets, full of dread,
I hovered on the confused area,
Autumn was coming in, the night air said.
Dark lady, car, and pizzeria.

I saw a universe in her black eyes
As she went by forever. My heart bled.
The pizza dough flew in the air. The cars
Were pretty smashed up, but nobody died.

Song for *The End of the Affair*

to bed you bring
sad as sad can
your worrying
you touch a man

and fingers touch
and veins unstart
the blood to such
and such a heart

four eyes close
and sorrow's eyes
relinquisu those
on your thighs

nor who would see
to see you then
Gethsemene
several men

the somber road
goes low goes high
each episode
occurs close by

and at your side
love and complaint
love crucified
suffering saint

Watching *Woyzeck*

you think it's life
you understand
but it's just the play
you understand
you understand

"Waiting for the Veil to Be Lifted"
—Roseanne Cash

It came down to a pissing contest with God
With me naked and up front
The shy Almighty
Doing his business behind a screen
And all I had going was the certainty of
Being able
To prove the proof flawed
You can't ever win
Reason's great that way
Allowing
To reason reason's flawed
And in the process
I befoul myself
Yet pee on

Reflections in a Jaundiced Eye

Unbeknownst to the unassuming beneficiary
It takes the body's zillions of arteries
And nerve endings
To set up the effortless ability
To will the arm to lift, it lifts

It's the nuclear resonance
That allows the periodic table
That allows RNA and DNA
And the iconic helix

Looking at a single leaf
And then an orchid . . .

And the surge of feeling welling

And still one wants the poem beautiful

Beauty the beautiful

Be You Tea Full

T.S., W.B., and The Beatles Answer Present at the Umpteenth Coming

This is the way lovemaking ends
This is the way lovemaking ends
This is the way lovemaking ends
With a bang, and a whimper

And, after the magical mystery mélée
Your eyes, your glittering eyes, are gay

Ars Poetica cum Apologia Pro Vitae Summa

No license!

The chutzpah

The shining

Rather than, A complex way to say a simple thing, the simplest way to say a complex thing

Beauty—for art's sake

Truth—for goodness sake!

Krapp's *spool*, Monsieur Krapp's *bobine*

Debussy: "You have only to listen. Pleasure is the law."

The World Is Everything

The world is everything that is the casket
The endlessness before the infinitude
The plenitude before the beginning
And ever and ever (and ever) on

Now, octopus, select your coral shells
On the sea's bottom
Not for want of a better blob in the continuum
But for very much the look the feel the color
The boneless eminence of you
I confer my homeless idea
On top your palpitating body

"What Good Is *I Love You* If It's the Answer to a Question?"

No claim here, dear student,
I've forgotten your name,
That the phrase is mine
I just don't want it to be lost
In a sea of forgotten lore
So all credit to you for coming up with it
And with it alone you join the ranks
As far as I'm concerned
With an entry in Bartlett's
Your sad poignant phrase proclaims
A truth so blazingly brazenly blatantly true!
What Good *Is* "I Love You" If It's the Answer to a Question?
The ear rebels, the heart
Shattered by the pitch alone.

Lucia

O Lucia, Laura-lost in the folds of memory,
How I met you, how you appear and disappear
In my porous recollections, a virgin still at forty,
A brazen sexuality you knew not what to do with,
Dragged back, drugged, to Italy by your sister, bride of
Lammermoor, forever Laura-lost in the folds of memory,
Mad Lucia, coloratura of involuntary forgetting
Where, where in the world might you dwell?

The Tongue at the Tower of Babel

At what point in the evolution of the language
of the still evolving species was the gene
for the visceral disapprobation of the mispronounced word implanted—
was it when orchids began to imitate butterflies
so that butterflies could mistakenly sip the flowery nectar,
thus assuring the perpetuation of orchids,
much to the delight of the biped species
violently and agitatedly reacting to the butchered utterance
of a word every decent person should know
how to pronounce properly?

Thank You, Roger Kimball, Thank You, Martin Filler, Respectively

Bafflement's my state
Given life's severity
As I try
Of late
Before I die
To negotiate
The pitiless "discipline of posterity"
The "ecumenical indifference of fate."

"The Lottery" Revisited

Go no further on that verdant knoll
than if you pick the Queen of Spades
from the cosmic crapshoot—
despite the mixed metaphor, thank you,
you are fucked, friend,
as neighbors gather round
in stone-throwing compassionate
Schadenfreudian pity

Memorabilia

Of the detritus clogging the porous brain
Most peculiarly this ninth grade anomaly survives—
I'm at the movies with the late Dan Aronoff
On Bernard Ave, watching *The Bullfighter
And the Lady*, Robert Stack the bullfighter
He of TV's *Unsolved Mysteries* fame
And best remembered for it though no longer
All that handsome as he's here bullfighting
Bullfighting's of course Hemingway's
Sanctioned butchery as the true poetic image
Of the times, writing itself over and over
In so many brave suicidal passes
As what the less brave turn away from
Death in the afternoon and at your typewriter too
Alas poor Manolete . . .

And all the while me enthralled
Enthralled with Stack, the lady, and the bull
Intent in fact from early on
To sit through a second showing
Which meant sitting through the second feature
(A double feature this), a lemon, that one, over again too

And, yes, the reason for the clogging,
The unfixable hurt that lingers?
Consider Danny (dead a long time, heart, died too young
On the operating table) not understanding why
Anyone would want to see a movie over again *that you've
just seen*—and me, having just come off *The Battleship
Potemkin* (maybe this part exaggerated, recruited recall
from another time), *serious* about film—
Consider Danny slowly reluctantly sadly indicating he
Was *not* ready to sit through two films again—
Indicating he was ready to leave, and he left.

Bio

Sigmund, brother
how is it
you said bad memories
are repressed
obsessive worries
suppressed,
would not be surface pleading
but lie buried deep
in the keep
of the subconscious needing
the most pliant pincer pliers
to dislodge the outliers—
how is it then
that when
I sit to pen my my oh
bio,
having lived a slice,
all I dredge up is what's *not* nice—
from the muck
of life's road
(my luck)
just one exquisite
painful episode
after another?

V. Allegretto

On Science and Art

Given the quality of the darkness
Who should care where the light comes from
Except that art illuminates in one way
Science in another
And the images they conjure up out of the darkness
Are vastly different
And suggest vastly different images beyond

So the explorers by these respective lights
Are inevitably betrayed
By the abstractest of occupational hazards
For the feeding back from image to eye
Re-educates the eye to what it sees
So that eventually only the thing seen
Can ever be seen

In art and science the differences affect all
The dreamer and the dream
The categories have become, remain
Two discrepant domains
Two visions of things
Two . . . sensibilities, wracked and distended
By reciprocal misunderstandings spilling into fear
The fear into abiding mutual suspicion
The reciprocal contradictions
Collecting in a bulging box

The bewitchment of language, one frames questions
For which there are no answers
One succumbs to the self congratulatory error
Of taking description for explanation
Prescription for cure

Self reference mirrors the most overwhelming
Of philosophical problems, what is the nature
Of self consciousness in the otherwise
Indifferent universe

In discord over the nature of the goal
And over how it is to be sought
Nonetheless
In precariously cantilevered edifices of self reference
The practitioners elaborate answers
All the while that they recognize
The discrepancy between the tools and the task

"The Free Man Thinks of Nothing Less Than of Death"
—Spinoza

Vacationing Descartes meets Spinoza
O the sublime, the unavoidable ambiguity of it
And will the free man start to think of *It*
When he isn't supposed to be thinking

And will he be less free therefore
And what pray tell is the thinking
Man otherwise thinkingly thinking of
Since only because he thinks, he is?

Port-au-Prince, January 2010
—for Debbie Folaron
I. Terra Firma

The Earth opens
gaping fissures
and countless bodies
fall
The Earth gives way
No terra firma
No world
beneath it all

the screams
deafening screams
louder silent screams
the reverberations
fill the Earth's canopy
never to go away
Oh my Haitian friends
thousands
thousands
dead
crevasses
crevices
the Earth spilling it guts

the equations say the sound
never goes away
you hear it ringing still

Oh my Port au Prince
your presence writ in bodies
decomposing in the sun
on the solid collapsed ground
that betrayed you.

II. Debbie's African Friend

African friend
I never met
I found a tragic poem
in your letter to Debbie—
I translate from the French:

This to tell you, Debbie, I'm back.
Sick, but glad to have done something.

I now have a fairly precise idea
What the end of the world will look like.

Just think, 90% of high schools, colleges,
Primary schools, public and private,
Have collapsed, killing everyone.
Government buildings tumbled,
Killing the civil servants.
The university is gone, killing the chancellor,
The professors, the students. The cathedral,
Gone, killing the archbishop and 23 priests.

A corpse doesn't talk.
It says nothing about its accomplishments or its education.
A corpse doesn't say, I'm a neurosurgeon,
Trained for 40 years in the best hospitals in the world.
A corpse, rotting in the sun.

Port-au-Prince emits an apocalyptic odor, of the end of time.

III. Voltaire

No accident Voltaire
chose the earthquake
that devastated Lisbon in 1756
to candidly blurt out
Heck, what's going on here—
What's the purpose, Lord Almighty—
So that, among the 200,000 dead, someone
picked from his cramped stone sarcophagus
buried alive for three days, can say
to reporters who ask,
The Lord was with me?

IV. Buddha Visits Haiti

Halfway up the lapis hill
a Buddha head
lies in the brush
by the roadside
the decapitated remnant of a dream
waking to gather in
the stench of rotted bodies
the bloodied rock and rubble
and emerge with a truth—
that suffering in the world
at any moment
was so immense
is too immense
for one mind to assimilate

Crazy Jane, Demotic
—Homage to Willliam Butler Yeats

Bumped into the Bish on Main
He didn't stop blabbering
Said my tits sagged, I'd better
Stop living like a slut
Or I'll never make it to heaven

Not so fast, I said

Good and bad are closer
Than you think
Good *needs* bad
My buddies are dead
I haven't screwed in years
Yet I still have my pride

My heart knows love
When it sees it, even if
Love shacks up in a shithouse
It's better for it
Since nothing's perfect
That doesn't have imperfect in it

Mr. Scott of Oakley Street, London

Mr. Scott, O Mr. Scott
you ought
not
to go out
in the cold
without
a coat
did not
your mother scold
you for same?
you'll catch your
death as it were
and who's to blame?
not her

The J, K, L Suite

I.
To fight the scourge
Of professional ecstasy
lovers are not innocent
in the purple rain;
feather hair cushions
the heavy heads
which, winning
knowledge, dash
against the sands.

I will not tell you
the fiber music
at your ears is not
a temporary song
or the burning
of my fever heart
will dominate the lengths
while acid shadows eat
earth inconsequentially;
passion doesn't
trap me to deceive;
I'm not innocent
I move cat eyed in
the perfumed darkness, the
curvature of my approach
as geometric as a wall;
sadness shapes my motion
to your side, my constant pain
hovers round your lips.

I know I have to ponder
the forever of
this love against the
ephemeral sun; but love

you as I do I'm not
robust as the sun; he'll
bomb with brightness the
crooked sheets
of the then empty bed

II.
lips
and eyes
black with sex
disturb an
elaborate scientist
and mock
the turgid
logic of
his brain

but I like
your havoc
love and
I will play
at games
that skewer
the blasted patterns
of my ordered
arithmetic

III.
Oh my love's a dancer
whose rhythmic ways
happily invade the privacy
we own

when together
our moody lovers'

silence
provides the music
for her ardent step

IV.
You are defined
by the black hair
that splans my mind
like the viscous air

a steady wonder to the boy
who dotes on you

who marks
but cannot match
by any experience
the miracle music
of your girlish laugh

The Marvin Story

Always eager with advice
I say, him patiently listening,
Black Box refers to a process
Or device
Whose output is of interest
(This is the test)
But whose inner workings
Are mysteriously
Not understood
As maybe the workings should

Not wishing to bore
I leap to seal the metaphor
I say, Alas, friend,
We're not
As you might think
A happy lot
On the outside
Looking *on*
And playing tricks.
In the end
Life has placed us, I fear,
Actually *in*
The Box
To which Marvin replied
In a blink
Yeah, and it's getting pretty
Sweaty
Down here.

Momento Mori

Momentos of the mori
Take on many forms
Among them the story
Of the restless curious Pharaoh
Who ordered a slave
Brought before him
Then ordered another
To beat the first
Within an inch of his life
As the wretch's life blood ebbed

The Pharaoh, frantic, watched
Knelt, shouted to the dead man
Tell me
What is death like?
What *is* death like?
What is *death* like?
Death . . .
No matter.

The slave with dying breath
And all the sadder
With firm resolve
Spat the mighty king
In the eye
Barely audibly uttering
Each man for himself
Must die

Macbeth Doth Murder

Battered by the waking world
I sought repose in dreams
Hopes of rest quickly derailed
Sleep isn't what it seems

Panic, terror, fear, and fright
Besieged my fretted rest
The day was traded for a night
By pitiless pain possessed

I slept, awoke, I slept, and then,
Prayed god my soul to keep
Only to confront again
The next assault of sleep

Short Story

a character
a character
the only one
come to think of it
who sitting in
a restaurant
sees a woman
two tables away
can't take eyes off her
everything seemingly
ineffably perfect
tremors of mind and body
accompanying the vision
(no question, the eyes
the eyes of the beholder
doing this)
only to return home
as happy as
perhaps happier than
he'd left that morning
to give his wife
an especially warm embrace

Mother

I think I'll take my mother on a cruise,
The weather's raw and there's no taming it.
Now at her age there's fickle time to lose,
No time to lose the chance time to outwit.

I think I'll take my mother on a cruise,
The dream is sweet and I keep dreaming on.
Oh, Mother, do not wake me with the news
That you're long gone, long gone, long gone, long gone.

Afterthought

Hail stranger stonemason
Across the centuries
Laboring at the base of St. Peter's
Who when asked, What are you doing?
Properly responded
I'm placing perfectly shaped stones
One atop the other
One above, one beside
As precisely as I can
Unlike his colleague who loftily answered
When asked same
I'm constructing a magnificent cathedral!

Myself I spend these days
Contemplating in blank verse
The epistemology
Of the eschatology
Recognizing alas too late
I'd have better spent my life in
The little time to spare
Devising a homage to the safety pin
Than building ratiocinative castles in the air

The Nature of Things

whereby I took one jump into the cool night
blasted off with at least a sense
of my evanescent identity
and landed somewhere
between Mercury and Mars
tumbling through space
sans fear
sans space capsule
vastness . . .
vastness left and right

stay away from cliché, friend
stay away
don't whistle in the dark

there's no more reason in the night
than the moon caught in a rain barrel
don't rail against the wind
that would direct you home
(if only you knew
where home was)

A Back Roads Route to Keats's Grand Concordance
—for Laurence Mintz

Of *how* one plays
What one says
Let me count the ways

Marry *manner* to *matter*
Poet
And so be it
Marshal *medium* to *message*
(The medium is the message, said he
Memorably)
And while you're at it
Admit
In the epistemological dance
Style trumps *substance*
And to avoid discontent
Let *form* transform *content*
Moreover let *means* prevail
When the *end*'s behind a veil

Now consider
Style/substance, manner/matter
Form/content, means/ends
Medium/message, how/what
How the whole lot
Ineluctably wends
To *Beauty* the *manner*
Truth the *matter*

And Keats's urn whispering a call
To all who gather whether friend or foe
Beauty *is* truth [italics mine], truth beauty, that is all
Ye know on earth, and all ye need to know.

Bagatelle in a Minor Key
—for Russell Connor

How could it be otherwise
How could it otherwise be
Green winged teal, butterflies

Contemplating the fiery sunrise
One aches to solve the mystery
How could it be otherwise

Lifeless staring plucked out eyes
Define ineffability
Green winged teal, butterflies

The truth beyond the border lies
In the vastness of eternity
How could it be otherwise

It's futile to philosophize
The journey risks ignominy
Green winged teal, butterflies

For hurt caused I apologize
In intimations of mortality
How could it be otherwise
Green winged teal, butterflies

Plainly Said

Plainly said
the not yet Buddha fled
faith and home
sickened by the shallow piety
of both
and walked, then jogged
through town
into the beckoning woods beyond
past stacks of banyans, mucalindas
and a *ficus religiosa*
before, exhausted now,
he fell asleep
under a pipal tree.

When he woke
he sensed to the exclusion
of every other thought
a truth invading his conscience—
that essential pain
wholly engulfed the world
more pain at any instant
than any one mind could grasp—
and all at once
legend has it
one hundred tiny Buddha heads
sprang from his forehead
to help him comprehend . . .

Once in a temple in Japan
I saw a giant Buddha head made of stone
bedecked with a ribbon of midget heads
gracing the brow
like so many cartoon beads of sweat
below which the immense carved countenance
looked down with an expression
of surpassing serenity

ABOUT THE AUTHOR

Morty Schiff has traveled around the world from East to West, thus losing a day in the life (but he's working hard to make up for it). He taught Mathematics and Creative Writing over many years, and squeezed in writing poems when the spirit spoke. He's lived in, and has been nurtured by, Montreal where he was born; Paris; New York; and Metuchen, New Jersey, where he presently resides with his wife Rebecca and daughters Amalia Jaclyn and Danisa Sarah.

Poetry Books from *Pleasure Boat Studio: A Literary Press*
(Listed chronologically by release date. *Note:* **Empty Bowl Press** is a Division of Pleasure Boat Studio.)

The Every Day. ~ Sarah Plimpton ~ $15.95
Hanoi Rhapsodies ~ Scott Ezell ~ $10 ~ an empty bowl book
Dark Square ~ Peter Marcus ~ $14.95
Notes from Disappearing Lake ~ Robert Sund ~ $15
Taos Mountain ~ Paintings and poetry ~ Robert Sund ~ $45 (hardback only)
P'u Ming's Oxherding Pictures & Verses ~ trans. from Chinese by Red Pine ~ $15 ~ an empty bowl book
Swimming the Colorado ~ Denise Banker ~ $16 ~ an empty bowl book
A Path to the Sea ~ Liliana Ursu, trans. from Romanian by Adam J. Sorkin and Tess Gallagher ~ $15.95
Songs from a Yahi Bow: Poems about Ishi ~ Yusef Komanyakaa, Mike O'Connor, Scott Ezell ~ $13.95
Beautiful Passing Lives ~ Edward Harkness ~ $15
Immortality ~ Mike O'Connor ~ $16
Painting Brooklyn ~ Paintings by Nina Talbot, Poetry by Esther Cohen ~ $20
Ghost Farm ~ Pamela Stewart ~ $13
Unknown Places ~ Peter Kantor, trans. from Hungarian by Michael Blumenthal ~ $14
Moonlight in the Redemptive Forest ~ Michael Daley ~ includes a CD ~ $16
Lessons Learned ~ Finn Wilcox ~ $10 ~ an empty bowl book
Jew's Harp ~ Walter Hess ~ $14
The Light on Our Faces ~ Lee Whitman-Raymond ~ $13
Petroglyph Americana ~ Scott Ezell ~ $15 ~ an empty bowl book
God Is a Tree, and Other Middle-Age Prayers ~ Esther Cohen ~ $10
Home & Away: The Old Town Poems ~ Kevin Miller ~ $15
Old Tale Road ~ Andrew Schelling ~ $15 ~ an empty bowl book
Working the Woods, Working the Sea ~ Eds. Finn Wilcox, Jerry Gorsline ~ $22 ~ an empty bowl book
The Blossoms Are Ghosts at the Wedding ~ Tom Jay ~ with essays ~ $15 ~ an empty bowl book
Against Romance ~ Michael Blumenthal ~ $14
Days We Would Rather Know ~ Michael Blumenthal ~ $14
Craving Water ~ Mary Lou Sanelli ~ $15
When the Tiger Weeps ~ Mike O'Connor ~ with prose ~ $15
Concentricity ~ Sheila E. Murphy ~ $13.95
The Immigrant's Table ~ Mary Lou Sanelli ~ with recipes ~ $14
Women in the Garden ~ Mary Lou Sanelli ~ $14
Saying the Necessary ~ Edward Harkness ~ $14
Nature Lovers ~ Charles Potts ~ $10
The Politics of My Heart ~ William Slaughter ~ $13
The Rape Poems ~ Frances Driscoll ~ $13

Our Chapbook Series:
No. 1: *The Handful of Seeds: Three and a Half Essays* - Andrew Schelling - $7 - nonfiction
No. 2: *Original Sin* - Michael Daley - $8
No. 3: *Too Small to Hold You* - Kate Reavey - $8
No. 4: *The Light on Our Faces*—re-issued in non-chapbook (see previous list)
No. 5: Eye - William Bridges - $8
No. 6: *Selected* New Poems *of Rainer Maria Rilke* - trans. fm German by Alice Derry - $10
No. 7: *Through High Still Air: A Season at Sourdough Mountain* - Tim McNulty - $9 - with prose
No. 8: *Sight Progress* - Zhang Er, trans. fm Chinese by Rachel Levitsky - $9 - prosepoems
No. 9: *The Perfect Hour* - Blas Falconer - $9
No. 10: *Fervor* - Zaedryn Meade - $10
No. 11: *Some Ducks* - Tim McNulty - $10
No. 12: *Late August* - Barbara Brackney - $10
No. 13: *The Right to Live Poetically* - Emily Haines - $9

From other publishers (in limited editions):
Desire - Jody Aliesan - $14 - an empty bowl book
Dreams of the Hand - Susan Goldwitz - $14 - an empty bowl book
The Basin: Poems from a Chinese Province - Mike O'Connor - $10 / $20 - an empty bowl book (paper/ hardbound)
The Straits - Michael Daley - $10 - an empty bowl book
In Our Hearts and Minds: The Northwest and Central America - Ed. Michael Daley - $12 - with prose - an empty bowl book
The Rainshadow - Mike O'Connor - $16 - an empty bowl book
Untold Stories - William Slaughter - $10 / $20 - an empty bowl book (paper / hardbound)
In Blue Mountain Dusk - Tim McNulty - $12.95 - an empty bowl book
China Basin - Clemens Starck - $13.95 - a Story Line Press book
Journeyman's Wages - Clemens Starck - $10.95 - a Story Line Press book

Orders: Pleasure Boat Studio books are available by order from your bookstore, directly from our website, or through the following:
SPD (Small Press Distribution) Tel. 800-869-7553, Fax 510-524-0852
Partners/West Tel. 425-227-8486, Fax 425-204-2448
Baker & Taylor Tel. 800-775-1100, Fax 800-775-7480
Ingram Tel. 615-793-5000, Fax 615-287-5429
Amazon.com or **Barnesandnoble.com**

www.pleasureboatstudio.com

How we got our name

... from *Pleasure Boat Studio*, an essay written by Ouyang Xiu, Song Dynasty poet, essayist, and scholar, on the twelfth day of the twelfth month in the renwu year (January 25, 1043):

> "I have heard of men of antiquity who fled from the world to distant rivers and lakes and refused to their dying day to return. They must have found some source of pleasure there. If one is not anxious for profit, even at the risk of danger, or is not convicted of a crime and forced to embark; rather, if one has a favorable breeze and gentle seas and is able to rest comfortably on a pillow and mat, sailing several hundred miles in a single day, then is boat travel not enjoyable? Of course, I have no time for such diversions. But since 'pleasure boat' is the designation of boats used for such pastimes, I have now adopted it as the name of my studio. Is there anything wrong with that?"
>
> Translated by Ronald Egan

www.ingramcontent.com/pod-product-compliance
Lightning Source LLC
Chambersburg PA
CBHW060457080526
44584CB00015B/1455